Praise for *Wild, Unfelt World*

In the first poem of this collection, poet Hillary Gonzalez posits the question 'am I a heathen?' That question sets a joyful pace for the rest of *Wild, Unfelt World*. Gonzalez introduces us to the manifold layers of the human condition by inviting us on a nature walk. Each poem – each a story in its own right – is a look into nature's role as a teacher of man. As we encounter flora and fauna, as we converse with deer flies and herons, we grow ever wiser about who we are as humans. You will return to this collection again and again.

> E. Doyle-Gillespie, MLA Johns Hopkins University, BCPS Literature Teacher, author of *Father of the Red Grotto Used Bookstore*

This sophomore collection is a tender love letter to the many natures surrounding us. *Wild, Unfelt World* is a lovely addition to the expansive world of ecopoetics. Through the motif of birds, the author offers such rare empathy in our capitalistic hellscape. Amidst the many questions and few answers, Hillary Gonzalez grounds us in the beauty of the mundane and the grief of paying attention.

> Tramaine Suubi, author of "phases" and "stages"

In *Wild Unfelt World*, Gonzalez picks you up with her talons and teaches you how to fly. This collection brings clarity to the smallest of birds and the biggest threats to their existence. Upon reading these poems, you'll realize that looking toward the sky is perhaps the most important thing you can do.

> Clint Bowman, author of *If Lost* and *Pretty Sh!t*

Wild, Unfelt World
Copyright © 2025 Hillary Gonzalez

Cover Art by Harla Bisbey, who can be found on Instagram at @bird_hag
Author Photo by Marco Gonzalez

The font used is Garamond
The cover font is Adobe Handwriting

All rights reserved. No duplication or reuse of any selection is allowed without the express written consent of the publisher.

        Gnashing Teeth Publishing
        242 East Main Street
        Norman AR 71960
        http://GnashingTeethPublishing.com

Printed in the United States of America

ISBN 978-1-966075-26-4

Non-Fiction: Poetry

Gnashing Teeth Publishing First Edition

Wild, Unfelt World
by Hillary Gonzalez

This book of poetry is dedicated to Arlene, who taught me the names of trees, how to sing down cows from the high fields, whose favorite movie was *The Wizard of Oz*, and who I miss every single day. I love you, Nana.

Thank you, Marco, my love and biggest supporter. Wilbur, whose floppy ears and kissable snoot kept me going on those late nights typing this manuscript.

Author Statement on Artificial Intelligence

At no part of my writing or creative process was A.I. used to create this book. Poetry is a uniquely human experience, and A.I. cannot have a human experience. Furthermore, Generative A.I. is stealing the jobs of the working class, artists, guzzling up our drinking water, and poisoning our air. As a writer, as a human who belongs to the working class, and as someone who loves this planet with my entire being, I implore you to stop using Gen A.I. I promise you, the work you create with your brain and hands, is so much more exciting than anything A.I. could "create."

Table of Contents

The Wren 1
Wild, Unfelt World 2
Heron Sisters 3
Frozen Peas 5
Blackberries At Noon 6
The Poet Considers the State of The World 7
The Egret 8
Deer Flies 9
Banner Over the Marsh 10
I Take It Back 11
The Loon 12
Time 13
Peace 14
Sentinel of the Marsh 15
Wisdom of Indigo Buntings 16
Harbor Seals 17
Wilbur In the Sun 18
Giving Life to The Phantom 19
Becoming 20
The Fool's Journey 21
The Power Outage 22
Companions 23
Open Eyes 24
Autumn Sings to the Bees 25
Antler Velvet 26
White Rhino, Sudan 27
Sunlight and Black Snakes 28
The Marsh Comes Alive 29
Vanishing Before Our Eyes 30
Morning On a Quiet Marsh 31
Prayers 32
Flash Flood 33
On Meadowlarks and Missed Opportunities 34
Dawn 36
Coreopsis 37
Let Us Go Out 38
Death 39
Extraordinary 40
I Took Wilbur to the Ocean 41
Pawpaws 42
A Murder of Crows 43

The Garter Snake 44
A Different Way to Be 45
The Nesting Hawk 46
Outside 47
Listening to October 48
The Last Dance of the Bluebirds 49
The Science of Birdsong 50

The Wren

A family of Carolina Wrens
has established their
chatty household in the tree
just outside my bedroom window.
Every morning now, they begin to stir
with the rising sun–
when their song sounds the sweetest,
and I am awoken to
begin my day with them.
How lucky we are,
to live in a world
where Wrens build their homes
so close to our hearts.

Wild, Unfelt World

Am I a heathen?
Some would say so.
This evening, I am called
to my front porch by the hooting
of a Barred Owl.
The owl is beautiful,
he is death on silent wings,
and yet he is vital to this place.

Once, when I was a wild thing,
running through the field on our farm,
I felt a stirring in my heart,
and I looked up.
A Snowy Owl perched on the fence
just across the field.

Is that you, God?
My feet, which had been running
with the exuberance of a child,
were suddenly halted by the
amber eyes of the owl, looking back at me.
The owl did not answer my question,
not as a human might.
But I felt its spirit
call back to me, *I am.*
The small child looked at the great bird.
The great bird looked at the child.
Then it was gone.

Am I a heathen?
Perhaps.
But I will tell you this,
I know of the Divine.

Heron Sisters

When I am birding,
especially when I am on
a well-traveled trail,
I am often asked why I am there.
I answer politely, *Oh, I'm here for the birds.*
Most of the time, I am greeted
by a look of confusion, as if there
are more wonderous things to see than birds.
A silly thought, really.
Today I am joined
by two very old friends.
Not my friends, but perhaps now
I can greet them should we meet
on this trail again.
These two have been friends
since their girlhoods, and I can see
how they are truly sisters.
They have paused beside me,
and I have pointed out
a Great Blue Heron as he cranes
his long neck and puffs up
his feathers for afternoon preening.
There are quiet gasps,
and one of them whispers her
astonishment, as if she's afraid
the wind will pick up the quiet
wonder in her voice,
carry it to the heron,
and he will fly away.
We stand together, watching
the great bird for several minutes.
Joggers pass by, too distracted
by the importance of exercising
to notice this gift of nature.
The heron finishes his
important work, and springs
from the branch, flying away.
A collective sigh of pleasure
passes between us, and we

turn to smile at each other,
as if we just shared
a beautiful secret.
Perhaps we did.

Frozen Peas

There is something about the way
geese fly through the sky
that calls to us so.
I watch the young geese at the lake,
their hungry and eager mouths
open and waiting for scraps of bread.
I will tell all I can,
of the damage bread can do
to wild geese–
how it deforms their wings,
leaving a creature which belongs
to the skies earthbound.
My heart cannot stand a
wild thing meant to fly
forever grounded–
watching each season
as the flock flies away.

Blackberries At Noon

It is noon, later than I
usually go to the fields,
but the sun high overhead
is warming the blackberry brambles.
Each new cane hangs heavy
and laden with dark ripe fruit.
I should have brought a jar,
but instead, I am plucking
each berry from the bush,
and savoring the sweet tang
of their purple and red flesh.
The Grackles in the trees above me
cackle and whistle,
as if to say,
save some for me!
I will, of course.
I am always thinking
of what we leave for the birds.

The Poet Considers the State of The World

I am standing waste-deep
in the tall grass of the field,
listening to a chorus of Field Sparrows.
Their high, bright song
carries on the afternoon breeze.
I should be watching the
Fourth of July Parades,
and cheering as each tinseled
float slowly rolls by,
but instead, I am standing
in my favorite field, wondering
how much longer
it will be designated for conservation–
before all the beautiful, lush acreage
is purchased to construct houses
that all look the same.
No character, no soul.
I would scream, but I don't want
to disturb the peace of the meadow.

The Egret

I often find myself
crying each time I see an egret.
This day, perhaps this very hour,
could be my last.
I will drink in the glorious
snowy white of its wings,
and the way the afternoon
sun sparks against
each wing tip.
If this is my last day,
they will say I died among friends–
among kindred spirits.

Deer Flies

I came to the tall grasses
of the marsh to photograph
the Seaside Sparrows today,
but had I not stopped to
swat at the relentless deer flies
buzzing around my head,
I might have missed
the whimsy of newly born dragonflies
dancing in the marsh grass
just beside me.
I almost missed the bright
iridescent blue and green
of their small bodies,
and the way they fly together
in such intricate synchronicities.

Thank you, Deer Flies,
for making me stop–
for making me notice.

Banner Over the Marsh

Little plane, trailing a banner
advertising car insurance,
how dare you fly overhead
and disturb the herons.
We were all enjoying a moment of peace.

I Take It Back

Curse you, deer flies,
and all your ilk.
The Grackles are cackling
at me from the pines.
I am currently being escorted
away from the marsh
by the persistent flies.
I must look so foolish
to them, waving my hat
near my face.
Back in the safety
of my car, I apologize.
I'm sorry, Deer Flies.
I know, even you
serve a purpose here.

The Loon

To Assateague once more.
I've come to photograph the ponies,
and perhaps some herons.
I pause for a while,
listening to the muffled crashing
of waves in the distance,
the House Wrens—so merry and
full of wonder for the day,
when I hear a haunting cry
which shatters the serenity of the marsh.

How can I describe to you
the call of the Loon?
The way it steals your breath
from your chest,
chills the blood.
Yet your heart
pounds with a glorious love
for this ghost of the marsh.
I have never seen a Loon,
and I still haven't today–
but I heard it

Time

Time goes on.
I know there will be a time
when the marsh
and the forests I love,
where my friends the birds
come to greet me
each time I visit,
will no longer be here.

But, let it be three hundred
years from now.
Five hundred.
One thousand.

Don't let my heart break
within my lifetime,
when I must watch
the growing heat
dry up the marsh,
and the forests all burn away.

I am not against Time.
I am a friend of Time–
one who understands it.
What I cannot understand
is having the power
to change the world,
and doing nothing.

Peace

If I sit in the marsh
long enough,
and allow the salty breeze
to fill my lungs
with each inhale.
I always carry
this place with me.

I inhale gratitude
and love of the natural world.

I exhale regret
and all disconnection from
this untamable place.

Sentinel of the Marsh

He sits atop his dead pine tree,
guarding over the marsh grass,
the mollusks deep within the mud,
and the small, twisted mangrove trees.
He spreads his wings
and puffs out his black wings
with little crowns of red,
and screams down at me.
Don't you know, I am a friend?
He cocks his head and lets out
another shrill trilling cry.
It's just as well.
He should always be wild.

Wisdom of Indigo Buntings

What does the Bunting know
that I do not?
Probably a lot, I answer myself.
The Bunting, with his cerulean
feathers–which are actually black,
knows there is no point
in worrying about tomorrow.
He only knows of the song
within his chest, that
bursts from him each morning
as he greets the rising sun.
He knows of the wind
that lifts him high into the sky,
and of the abundance
of sunflower seeds in the field
where I now stand.
He knows of little,
and that is enough for him.
Today, my meditation
is how to be more
like the Indigo Bunting.

Harbor Seals

Like ripples of delight, moving gracefully
and playfully through the cold harbor
of Portland, Maine, came a pair of Harbor Seals.
It was our honeymoon, and we sat
eating "the best lobster rolls in Portland."

All my life, I have wanted to see a seal–
to watch it glide and frisk
through the water.
I don't know if you'll understand
the jolt of joy that raced through my heart
when each sleek shape emerged to show
their beautiful gray dappled heads.
I was on my feet,
crying out and pointing to my love.

I looked around to see who I could
share in this moment with.
Moments of such pure delight
are meant to be shared,
but then I realized to every other
diner in the restaurant,
the appearance of the seals
was just another Tuesday.
They did not see them
for the miracle they were.

May I never live a life
where seals become ordinary.

Wilbur In the Sun

Our back patio is drenched
in the delicious golden light
of the afternoon sun.
This is Wilbur's favorite time of day.
He stands by the back door,
telling me with his
soft brown dog eyes
to let him out in the world,
to let him soak up
as much of the sun
as his small body desires.
I open the door,
and Wilbur trots to
his favorite bit of warm rock.
My husband and I
call this his Lizard Time.
I often watch the happiness
that spreads over his whole body
as he sits in the warmth of the day.
Occasionally, he lifts his large square head
to sniff the messages on the wind
that only he and other animal kid can read.
For Wilbur, this is all the
happiness the world needs to hold–
he has the sun, warm rocks,
and his people love him.

Giving Life to The Phantom

I don't want to live like this,
my heart screams from behind my ribcage.

The machine keeps turning,
and we're all just waiting
to become caught in one of the cogs.
Yet, I know from the very depths
of this companion phantom
we call the soul,
that I was not meant for this life.

Where does your spirit belong?
Where do you go back to?

I am chasing a more vital
sort of existence, where my
spritely soul is fed daily
in the wonder I feed it.
Can you feel the wild spaces
calling out to you?
Do you not hear the Whippoorwill
as the sky turns indigo, and the
sun and the moon are balanced
together on opposite sides
of the scale of the sky?

Can you not feel the shriek
of the vixen as she calls
in the wilds of the field?

This, I think, is what
we were meant to be a part of.
I do not want to feel
my vitality slipping away,
as I must continue to sell the strength
of my very bones, in order to live.

Becoming

At the end of it all,
this body I once called home
will cease to be–
yet the fawn, the owl, and the fox
will go on without me.
What will I become, I wonder?
Will I become the bluebird
as my Nana joked she would become?
Will I become the hawk
soaring higher as each updraft
catches the razor edges of my wings?
Or will I become the Willow
by the pond where the heron
comes to hunt?
When Death reaches out his hand to me,
I will not be frightened.
After all, haven't I seen him
in the woods, fields, meadows,
and mountains I often wander?

What will you become
when the arms of Death
are open to you?

The Fool's Journey

How foolish I was
when I was younger,
to wish to grow up.
Now, I am striving to
make my spirit young again,
by eating the blackberries
and wineberries I find
ripened on their thorny canes,
and by walking barefoot
over stream beds
when I look for salamanders.
The world is full
of too many adults.
What we need now are
the ones who refuse to grow up.
The ones who see what
our hearts could become
if the world wasn't
so consumed by promotions
and new sales goals.
The world needs you, darling.
Find what makes you
feel like a child again,
and hold onto it
with all your might.

The Power Outage

A great thunderstorm blew through,
taking our power with it
as its winds lashed at tree branches.
I was angry at first–being stuck
with the heat of the day,
but then we opened the windows
as the storm passed,
and suddenly I heard
the night blossoming into being.
The owls called from the woods,
declaring their territory,
and their young answered,
learning from their wise parents.
The little tree frogs sang
as though their hearts might burst
with the joy of awakening and
discovering night had come.
The power will come back.
Until then, I will bathe in
the glory of this summer night.

Companions

I have planted basil and marigolds
near my tomatoes to fend off the aphids
and the ever-hungry horn worms,
but I still know even the cucumber
and squash beetles are sustenance for
some small creature, who will thank me
for leaving a few plants where
they can also find the bounty in my garden.

Plant garlic for aphids.
The twisting tendrils and delicate
blossoms of nasturtiums will keep
the caterpillars from my brassica.
Sunflowers and corn give natural support
for my quickly growing pole beans.
If I plant dill, the small but fierce
lady bugs, will come to defend my tomatoes.

But still, I leave some plants for the "pests."
I know all things have a place in this world.
I must allow even my garden
to become part of the natural world.

Open Eyes

When I walk through this world,
through the fields or the forests,
I try to keep my eyes open.
I don't mean that I watch my steps
to keep from stumbling.
In truth, I am often stumbling.
My eyes are too busy looking skyward
on the bright mark of the Goldfinch,
than to watch where I put
my clumsy human feet.
In the fields, just beginning
to sing their promise of autumn,
I will stop and listen,
touch the long stalks
of goldenrod, just beginning
to burst through the field
as a wave might crash into the sand
sweeping the green away
in a sea of gold.
Too often, I have seen so many
oblivious to the unfolding joy
the world is offering us all.
When the fledgling Bluebird
with its chest still speckled
in the down of its youth,
is painted more and more blue
with the changing seasons,
I want to be there to witness
its first flight south.
I don't want to miss the present
being stuck in the past.
Are your eyes open?

Autumn Sings to the Bees

What tells the honeybee
autumn is approaching?
Is it the sudden heady scent
of wingstem and goldenrod?
Do the birds at dawn
sing of the new chill in the air,
even as they lose their summer
brightness from once vibrant feathers?
As each season fades into the other,
I watch each worker hurriedly
dance from one bud to another,
laden down in thick woolen
skirts of late summer pollen.
Where did the time go?
I was only just yesterday,
it seems, watching the fledgling
Cardinal in my backyard
open his mouth to
receive life from his parents–
who so often adorn my fence.
Now he shines crimson,
and autumn is coming.
At least I will still see him
as my breath clings to the air
and the wheel turns once more.

Antler Velvet

He stands within a clearing of trees.
The forest, thick with oak, beech, and poplar,
parted their trunks and roots
allowing him to shine in the
warm light of the afternoon.
Velvet gore hangs in ribbons
from his newly bone-white antlers.
No longer a fawn,
the white spots of his youth
are now the tawny brown
of dried grasses in autumn.
Men with guns will hunt
him through these woods,
counting each tip of his antlers,
exclaiming what a prize he is.
Keep running, and don't stop,
Little Brother.
Become the fabled old man
of the forest, with antlers
greater than those of your cousins, the elk.
I want him to live,
as I want for all wild things–
to be free.

White Rhino, Sudan

The last male northern white rhino died.
Once, they were perhaps as numerous
as blades of grass on the Savannah,
but now they are gone.
In cold, scientific terms,
they are known as "effectively extinct,"
as only two females remain.
We watched their numbers fall.
They were an acceptable sacrifice,
so, man could profit–
so, the West could profit.
How fitting, that his name was Sudan.
I watch the herons fly over the marsh.
In my lifetime, will I read the news
that the last heron has died?
In my niece's time?
In her children's time?
What will be the next casualty?
What would you do, to protect
the creatures with no voice?

Sunlight and Black Snakes

Too occupied by what was above me,
I nearly stepped on him.
His body is long and black,
gloriously scaled, and he rears up
as if he would strike me–
as if he were one of
his venomous cousins.
I'm sorry, Little Brother, I say.
You're right, of course.
I should pay more attention
to what's all around me,
and I swear I do–
but just now I was fixated
on the way the light
gently filtered through oak leaves.
The days are growing shorter,
you see, and the light
as I see it now, will
never be the same.
The black snake admonishes me
as though he might say,
look at me.
You see me as I am now,
but perhaps the next time
I will not be the same.
He is right, of course.
I will take it all in
while I still can.

The Marsh Comes Alive

Only a few weeks ago,
so short in the understanding of things,
the rising sun was greeted by
the reverent songbirds.
It is only the stalwart gull
who laughs and shrieks occasionally,
signaling the marsh isn't completely silent now.

I have sat, watching the first morning's light
touch the silvery wings of
the egrets and the ibis as they fly,
missing my friends, the Red-winged Blackbirds,
when suddenly a trumpeting fills
the sky like the Horn of Gabriel.

The geese have come.
They call and trumpet,
filling the sky just
as the light of morning
does each day,
and the marsh awakens.

The gulls, clapper rails, and herons
begin to call back.
Are they wishing them luck
just as I am?
Do they feel a wild kinship
just as I do?

I say a silent prayer for the geese
as each raucous "V" flies overhead.
Prayer connects us.
In this way, aren't we all one?

Vanishing Before Our Eyes

How do I tell her?
She reaches her still
chubby little fingers out
towards the fluttering monarch
as it alights from flower to flower.
I tell my niece to be gentle,
not only for the sake
of the fragile little being,
but also because
we have so few left.

So, how do I tell her?
How do I tell her
that in her lifetime,
we will see the monarch
become extinct?

A few years from now,
when she is older,
will she believe me
when I tell her that
when I was a child,
the skies, gardens, and fields
were full of monarchs
every late summer and autumn?

How do we tell all our children
that this was our fault?
How do I tell her?

Morning On a Quiet Marsh

The sun is rising over the marsh
like the reddest, juiciest summer tomato,
though the birds have already begun
their southern sojourns.
The reeds are all silent,
but the faithful wind still
quietly sings through the pines.
The wind will stay here
through every season.
The Kingbird and Red-winged Blackbird
have all gone with the rest
of the summer songbirds.
From somewhere in the marsh,
a shorebird begins to sing
its metallic clacking song,
and though I cannot see them
from where I stand,
a choir begins all around me.
Answering calls of
Hello!
Good morning!
I am here too!
The gulls chime in,
not apt to be forgotten,
and I am no longer alone here.

Prayers

I wonder how fox in the meadow prays.
A human might pray for more money,
but perhaps the fox only prays
for the sun to rise each day,
and that he finds the mouse
to fill his belly.
The fox already knows
he is a part of whatever we
might call holy in this world.

I can tell you of the institutionalized
prayer I was brought up on,
which left me feeling empty
and full of shame,
or I could tell you how
I came to heal my spirit.
I could tell you how even Jesus knew
that to be near the true divine,
is to know our place is not in the temple.

It's here, in this marsh.
It's in the way the wind
speaks with a gentle voice
through the tall grass.
It's in the way the geese call to one another.
It's in the way the salmon that
return to the river to spawn
year, after year, also bring gifts
with them from the sea, to heal the land.

I could tell you these things,
but you're too busy plotting
your mastery of the land,
than to learn how to listen
to the voice that's been calling you back.

Flash Flood

Unencumbered, and running faster
than stampeding horses,
the river roils down
cement sidewalks and asphalt.
The banks of the river
were once held back
by a generous growth of trees,
whose roots thirstily drank
even the heaviest of rainstorms.
But now, for the sake of houses
that all look the same,
they've been uprooted.
Now we have concrete,
which cannot drink the rain.
We destroy the forests,
then wonder why it floods.

On Meadowlarks and Missed Opportunities

Each new birding season,
when my brightly feathered friends
feel the promise of spring
in the mysteries of their hearts,
I have been searching for the Meadowlark.

I saw one once.
It sat on a fence on the side of the road,
taunting my lack of camera.
Now, I have come back
to my favorite marsh to watch
the herons, terns, and plovers.
Among the shrieks of the
Red-winged Blackbirds,
a new song has split the morning.

The Meadowlark!

I have my camera today, but it seems—
like its cousin—this one taunts me too.
I cannot find it, but I hear its song
piercing the marsh with its
high and luxurious voice.

I want to capture an image of
the Meadowlark, so that I might
share its beauty, so that others
might see it and say,
yes.
This creature is worth saving.
Its home is worth protecting.

Perhaps I was meant only to
listen as the bird's song pours
into the crevices of my very being.
Perhaps I was meant to write down
how my breath caught
and tears sprang to my eyes
as I listened with an open heart

to the glorious bird.

Have you ever heard such joy
in all your life, as the song
of the Meadowlark?

Dawn

My favorite time to be
out in the woods and marshes
is before the world wakes up.
The sun is gently blooming,
a Tiger Lily unfurling its petals,
blossoming along the horizon.
Birdsong sounds the sweetest
before the humidity of the day
dampens their song.
It is the time of day
where I can simply *be*,
and allow myself to observe
unencumbered by obligations
of the mind, when I only want
to feel what feeds my spirit.

What I want in this world,
is to feel my spirit opening
like the petals of a newly budding rose,
or perhaps the daisy in the field.
I will not find this feeling behind walls–
or looking out of windows.

It is here,
in the wildness of trees
and grass, that I feel
my soul singing.

Coreopsis

I can hear an Eastern Towhee
in the field just ahead
lined with pine trees.
Their citrus and lusty scent
fills the meadow.
I could walk through the field,
but I would disturb the red clover,
which has grown tall
alongside the sunshine yellow
medallions of wild coreopsis.
I could walk through the field,
but I think today I was simply
meant to watch as the
Purple Martins and
Barn Swallows dive and swoop
over the wildflowers,
delighting in this world
and the field that's been
set alight by the glories of summer.

Let Us Go Out

I must sell my youth
for the sake of living.
I must toil until my limbs are spent,
and my heart is worn out.
But this isn't how
it was supposed to be.

I was meant to bathe my skin
in the incandescent glow
of the rising full moon.

I was meant to awake
early in the day,
drinking in birdsong
as though I had
walked through the desert
with a terrible thirst.

I was meant to stand
ankle deep in streams,
watching butterflies
leap from puddle to puddle–
drinking in the earth.

Come with me.
Come with me to the wild spaces.
Come with me, and I will
show you where we belong.
Where *you* belong.

Death

I saw Death in the field today.
He was not stalking,
as so many are apt
to describe him.

Death was beside the soft-furred
rabbit lying in the field,
waiting to die.

Death was not haunting
the rabbit as it lay bleeding
out its lifeblood.

Death reached out one
shrouded hand, and stroked
the long ears lovingly.

I sat and watched
as the rabbit slipped away.

In this world,
I know we must hold onto
the things we love most,
while we still can.

Death is always there,
but not as a ghoul.
Death is a teacher,
a friend,
a lover.

Death was with the rabbit
as it caressed it into
this new journey through darkness.

Death will be there for me too,
when I am ready.

Extraordinary

Let nature take its course.
How many times
have you heard that?

What if you learned,
remembered,
knew, were part of nature?

Understand this, Dear One–
have you ever seen the flash
of a hawk as it strikes
at its prey in a blaze of talons,
and thought to yourself,
Oh! How extraordinary?

What if I told you
that it is not extraordinary,
but rather everyday blessings?

Would you believe me if I told you
the sight of a falcon,
hawk, or even the screeching
Blue Jay, could be yours
if you only learned
to look once more?

The world needs you to remember
you are a part of it.

I Took Wilbur to the Ocean

I rolled the windows down
so he could take in the new smells all around him—
so he might know the ocean as a friend
before he was introduced to it.
His nose greedily took in the salt and brine of the air
as the gulls shrieked their greetings overhead.

On the beach, Wilbur felt the warmth
of sand heated by the afternoon sun
on his paws for the first time.
He danced over the sand.
Perhaps it was the sound of the waves,
or this new sensation beneath his paws,
but suddenly there was such joy
which spread over his whole body.

I brought him to the edge of the water.
As each new wave cascaded over the sand,
Wilbur jumped away, then ran back
when the water spilled around his small legs.
Then, he was overcome with the thrill
of the day:
the sun,
the sand,
the coolness of water,
and he began to run in circles
around my feet.
He pulled his lips back in
a wide smile as he ran
and skipped around me.

I wondered if I had ever felt
such happiness in all my life
as my little dog.
I wonder, what would life be like
if we tried to see the thrills
of this world as Wilbur does?

Pawpaws

September danced into October
with the joys of late harvests
and the new becoming that is
the changing of seasons—
even as this one is dying.

I have been watching
the Pawpaw trees
in the forests and pathways
I walk every day.

I have been watching the
red flowers blossom,
calling to the flies and beetles
to be pollinated.

I am waiting to taste the
vanilla custard of the Pawpaw fruit.

I could hide these trees away,
tell no one, and keep this
treasure to myself,
but I know these joys
are meant to be shared.

Join me.
Let me show you the bark
of the Pawpaw,
the wide tropical leaves,
so you might know it too.

Let me share this knowledge with you,
as it was meant to be shared.

A Murder of Crows

July.
The crows in my neighborhood
are in a frenzy today.
Two large dark shapes circle a pine tree
cawing and calling relentlessly.
A smaller voice, higher and sharper, calls back.
I can see the young crow
perched high, at the very top
on the small branches of the pine,
where the limbs lean over
with the weight of the juvenile.
Its parents circle, dive, and swoop,
calling all the while.
Come!
Fly!
Join us!
Join the dynasty of the sky!
I am blessed with this
observation today–
this new becoming.
This may be the most
important thing I do today.
I once saved a crow
in my neighborhood
whose wing had been broken.
I wonder now, as I watch
this new brood begin
their journey of flight,
Is this my crow's little darling?

The Garter Snake

I've paused on the dirt trail
with my sibling and brother-in-law.
We stand in a triangle,
like a protective living barrier
as the garter snake slips
its red clay and umber body
in and out of the sea of grass
it wades its lithe body through.
Two hikers pass by,
and they pause to ask
what we are so fascinated by.
My brother in law,
perhaps recognizing the fear
he might induce by announcing
the presence of the snake,
first holds his hands slightly apart
to signify how small–
how tiny this little being is,
before calling attention
to the little snake.
The hikers scurry away.
The word snake has
been said aloud.
I think to myself, how
strange it is, the reactions
we have to the creatures
of this world.
One group pauses to marvel
while the other runs in fear.
All things in this world,
no matter how venomous
or docile, only want to live.

A Different Way to Be

What I feel in my spirit
is so different from what
society wants of us.
You should know this about me—
I am always thinking
about my soul,
yours too, and how
all of us were meant
for so much more
than what we're given.
Do you feel it too?
Are you not also
screaming within
yourself to be free?
If I could lie all day
on a bed of moss,
breathing in the air
gifted to me by oaks and poplars,
I would be content.
This world wants, needs,
for us to rail against
the greed that presses in
from all sides.

The Nesting Hawk

In the spring, a Red-shouldered Hawk
made a nest across the street,
and sometimes while I sat in front of
of my computer, pretending I
cared about the contents of
of an email, I'd hear her fierce screams.
I watched her bring branch after branch
to an old sycamore,
then tenderly move them into place
with talons and beak
that had ripped through so many prey.
I watched her become a mother–
saw the tenderness in the
ruffling of her feathers
as she sat over her hatching eggs,
even in the heaviest of downpours,
to give her young her body's warmth.
In those moments, I wanted to
go to her nest and say,
watch my stomach grow.
Here, see? I am a mother too.
I cannot give life like the Hawk
who creates but also takes life.
Does that only make me a taker?
But you do create, says the Hawk.
You can teach your nieces
to be kind to creatures like me,
and isn't that helping give life?
In time, I hope to be able to
accept the lesson of the Hawk.
For now, I can allow myself to grieve.

Outside

Outside my office window,
the rays of the sun are singing,
calling me to enjoy perhaps
one of the last warm days of autumn.
You won't find what you're
searching for at your desk,
it calls out to me.
I know, I call back.
But, my heart is weary
with matters of commerce.
Every day, I wish with all my heart
to be more present,
to listen, I mean *truly* listen
to what even the little House Finch
is offering me from the depths of its heart.
The sun wants to share this
profundity with me.
Who am I to deny the sun?
Who are any of us to not accept
what's being offered?
I stop typing, and step out
into the light.
Today, the changing seasons
are more important.

Listening to October

October is begging me to pay attention.
I'll be gone soon, it whispers through its
kaleidoscope of carotene leaves.
As each day passes,
October tells me to slow down.
Each day I wake,
October is different.
The leaves are more bright,
the birdsongs are foreign and exciting,
until they've faded away.
October asks us to be silent
and appreciate what we have
when we have it.

The Last Dance of the Bluebirds

In the quiet meadow,
the Red-winged Blackbirds
once shrieked in summer,
from within stalks
of previously vibrant goldenrod.
The flora had been waiting patiently for autumn,
so they could shine in gilded splendor.
The oat grasses and rudbeckia
have heard the same whispering
voice of winter on the wind,
and are fading away too—as autumn
bids the earth farewell.
November will soon be upon us.
But just now, the Bluebirds are
dancing through the meadow, and
don't seem to mind the frost
that lingers longer each morning.
I count each bright blue shape
as they dance together
for perhaps one more time,
before they too leave the meadow
for warmer fields and trees.
There are so many, I wonder—
if I am still enough, would
they come to land on me?
I could be sad, and wish they'd stay,
but each spring, the Bluebirds
never break their promise
to come back to me.

The Science of Birdsong

A few years ago, scientists discovered
the effects of birdsong on our mental wellbeing.
They called it Attention Restoration Theory.
I often wonder about how
the study was conducted.
Did they have the participants hooked
to wires while strolling through a park,
or did one intrepid scientist
practice feeding the birds daily,
and realized how the chirping
of a Goldfinch brought peace
to an otherwise troubled mind?
I wonder, how we can
discover we were meant to
be in nature–that nature
lowers our blood pressure,
reduces stress, and still think
we are separate or even above
the natural world?
Birdsong has saved me.
I exist in a world that is all times
at odds with my brain chemistry.
Yet, when I am among the birds,
I no longer feel like an outsider.
I am in a space I belong,
where my mind is meant to be.
There are no harsh lights,
no incessantly loud noises
that make me feel like
I need to run away.
There is only me, the wind,
and the incandescent joy of birdsong.

About the Author

Hillary Gonzalez (they/she) is a queer, genderfluid, wildlife photographer, and AuDHD eco-poet and activist, whose work explores themes of identity and healing. Writing from the unique perspective of a birder, Hillary's poetry draws deeply from personal experiences in forests, marshes, and mountains–weaving together reflections on the natural world with a call to protect it. Growing up on a farm in the foothills of the Blue Ridge Mountains in Virginia, it was there where Hillary's love of nature was kindled. They are the author of the poetry collections, *Seasons, Wild, Unfelt World* (Gnashing Teeth Publishing), and *Where the Osprey Nest* (Palewell Press). Their poems have been published by South Broadway Press, Canid Press, and in the following anthologies: *Bi All Accounts* (Bi+ Book Gang) , *Unfurl* (Yellow Arrow Publishing), *In Praise of Despair* (Beyond the Veil Press), *The Body Archive* (Cosmic Daffodil Journal), and *Understory* (Loblolly Press), a fundraising zine to benefit the victims of Hurricane Helene. Hillary lives in Baltimore, Maryland, with their husband and dog Wilbur, where they continue to connect with readers on the intersections of neurodivergence, queerness, disability, and environmental advocacy. As a survivor of domestic violence and CSA, Hillary also strives towards connecting with other survivors, and helping them on their healing journey.

You can follow Hillary on Instagram and Threads, at @hillarygonzalezpoetry. On Facebook, at www.facebook.com/hillarygonzalezpoetry.

If you would like to experience the music Hillary listened to while writing *Wild, Unfelt World*, search for the "Wild, Unfelt World" playlist on Quobuz (an alternative to Spotify).

Book Club Questions

1. After *Wild, Unfelt World*, is there a place in your own life that you feel more connected to? A bird, tree, or moment? What memories of connection did the book stir up for you?

2. The title *Wild, Unfelt World* suggests something both emotional and elusive. What do you think "unfelt" means in relation to the book title?

3. In what ways do birds act as messengers or metaphors throughout the collection? What roles do they play beyond being part of the natural backdrop?

4. "May I never live a life where seals become ordinary" is one of the book's lines. What does this mean to you? How do we keep wonder alive?

5. What does the book suggest about the role of awe in activism and stewardship? How might wonder be a form of resistance?

6. What role do grief and loss play in the collection? How are they held alongside joy and reverence?

7. Many poems were written during birding walks. How does that shape the voice, pace, and perspective of the book? Do you feel like you're walking alongside the poet?

8. How does the book change the way you view the natural world around you? Did it make you notice something you hadn't before?

9. What poem in the collection resonated with you most deeply, and why? Was it an image, a memory it stirred, or a truth it revealed?

10. In what ways does *Wild, Unfelt World* redefine what it means to be in relationship with the land? How does it go beyond the idea of "saving nature" to emphasize mutual connection?

11. One of the poet's least favorite phrases is, "let nature take its course." After reading *Wild, Unfelt World*, how does that phrase work in opposition to the theme of the book?

12. Which poem challenged your way of thinking the most? Was there a moment where the poet's perspective surprised or unsettled you?

13. What emotions does the book stir up about climate change and environmental degradation? Does it leave you with despair, hope, or something else entirely?

14. The collection often blurs the line between the human and more-than-human world. How does this perspective shift your understanding of identity or place?

15. Did the book inspire you to take any personal action? Whether it's walking a new trail, supporting conservation, or just noticing the birds in your neighborhood—what stayed with you?

16. After reading *Wild, Unfelt World*, what acts of stewardship do you plan to enact in your own life–no matter how small. **Bonus**: share this answer with the author on their website. Your answer will be used in writing and art pieces.

www.ingramcontent.com/pod-product-compliance
Lightning Source LLC
LaVergne TN
LVHW050029080526
838202LV00070B/6980